This Coloring Book Belongs To

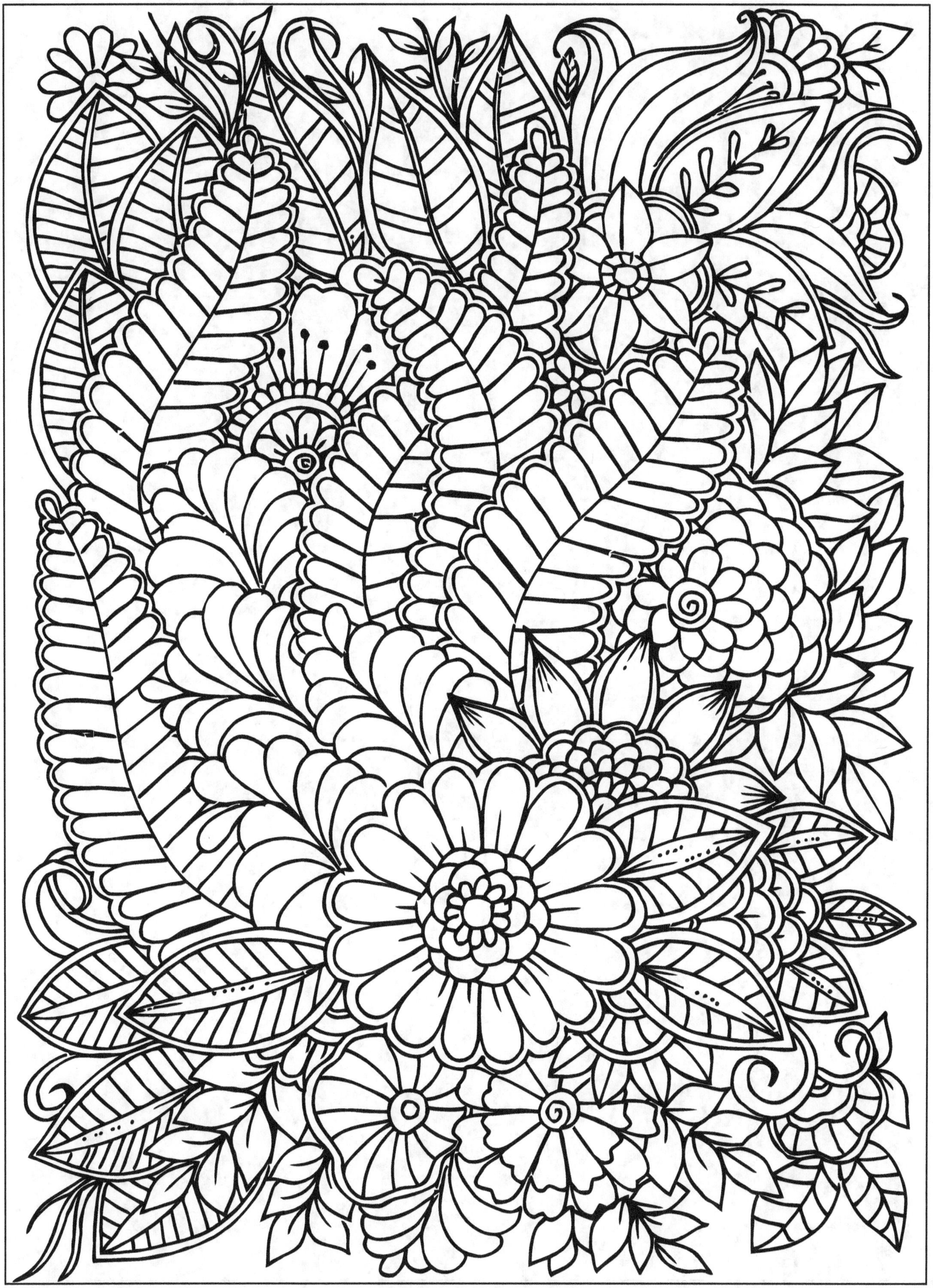

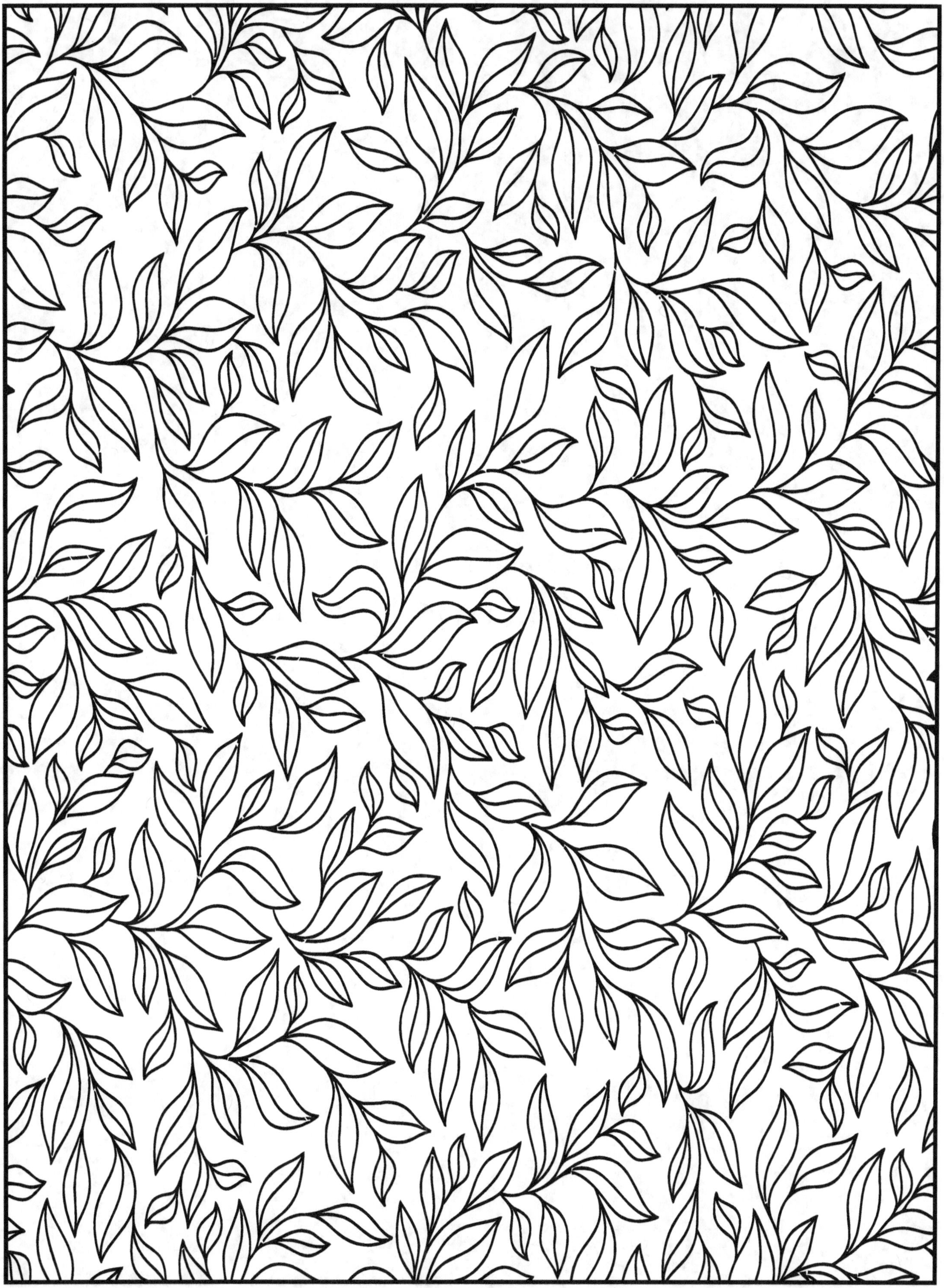

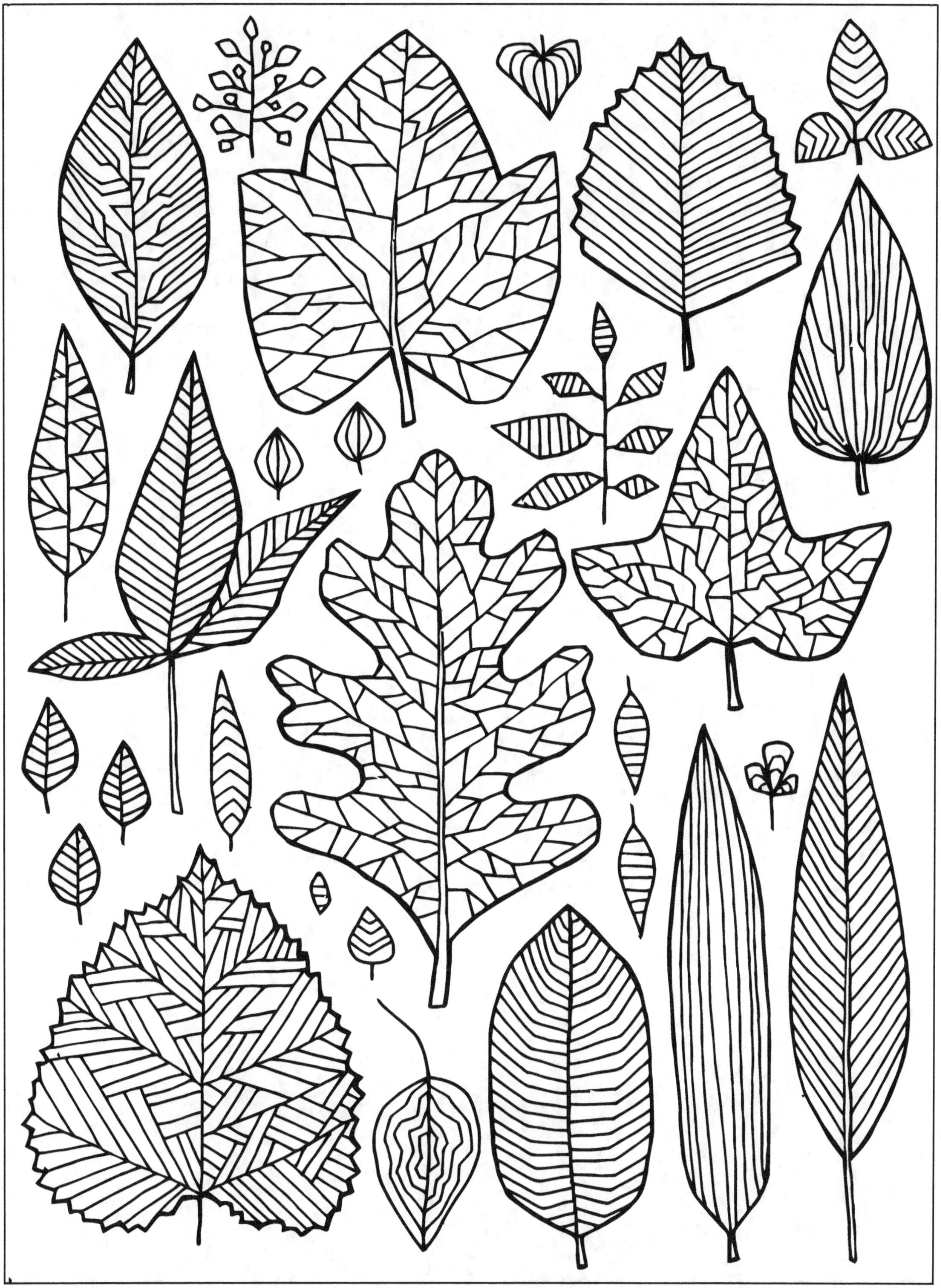

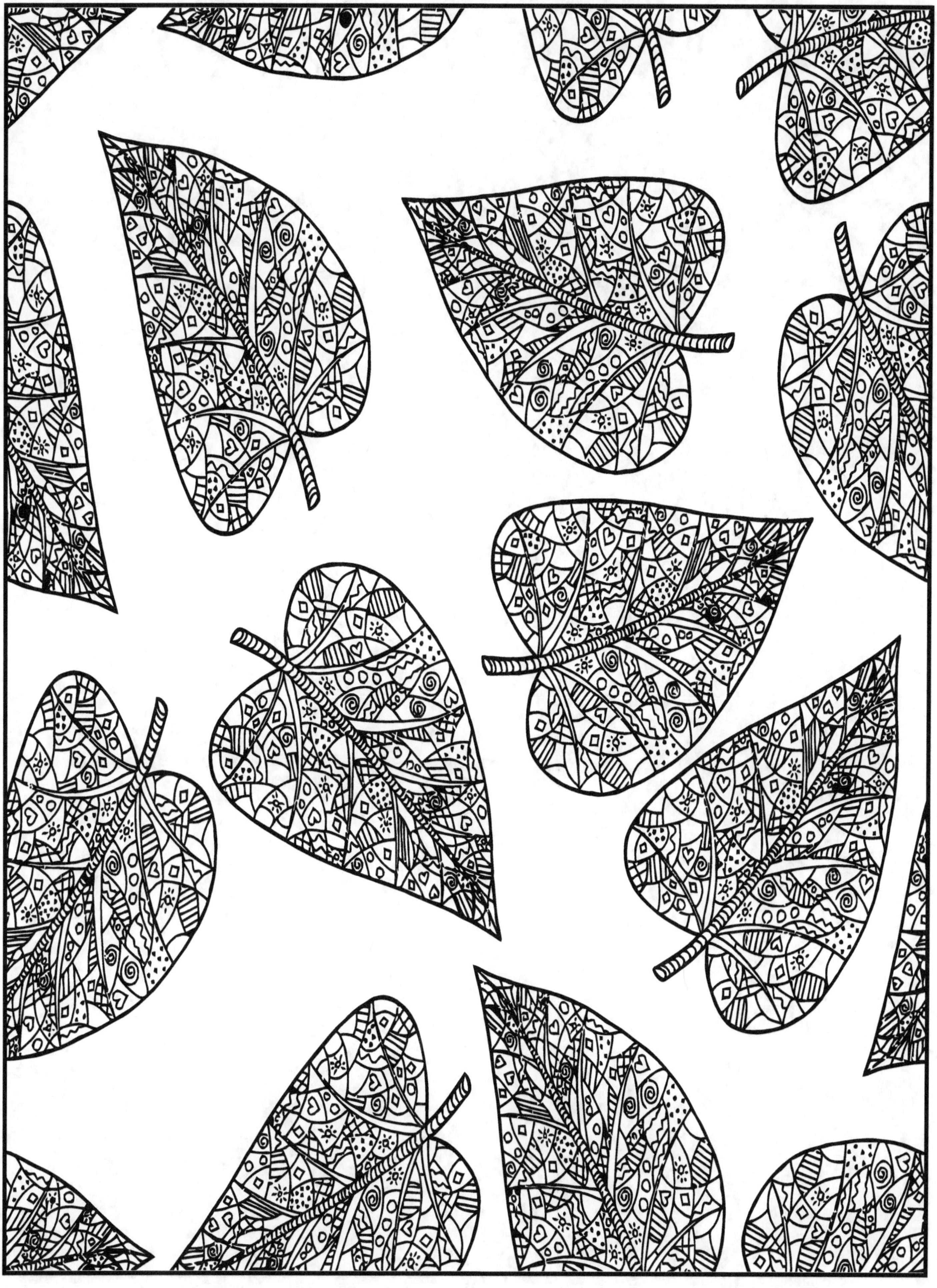

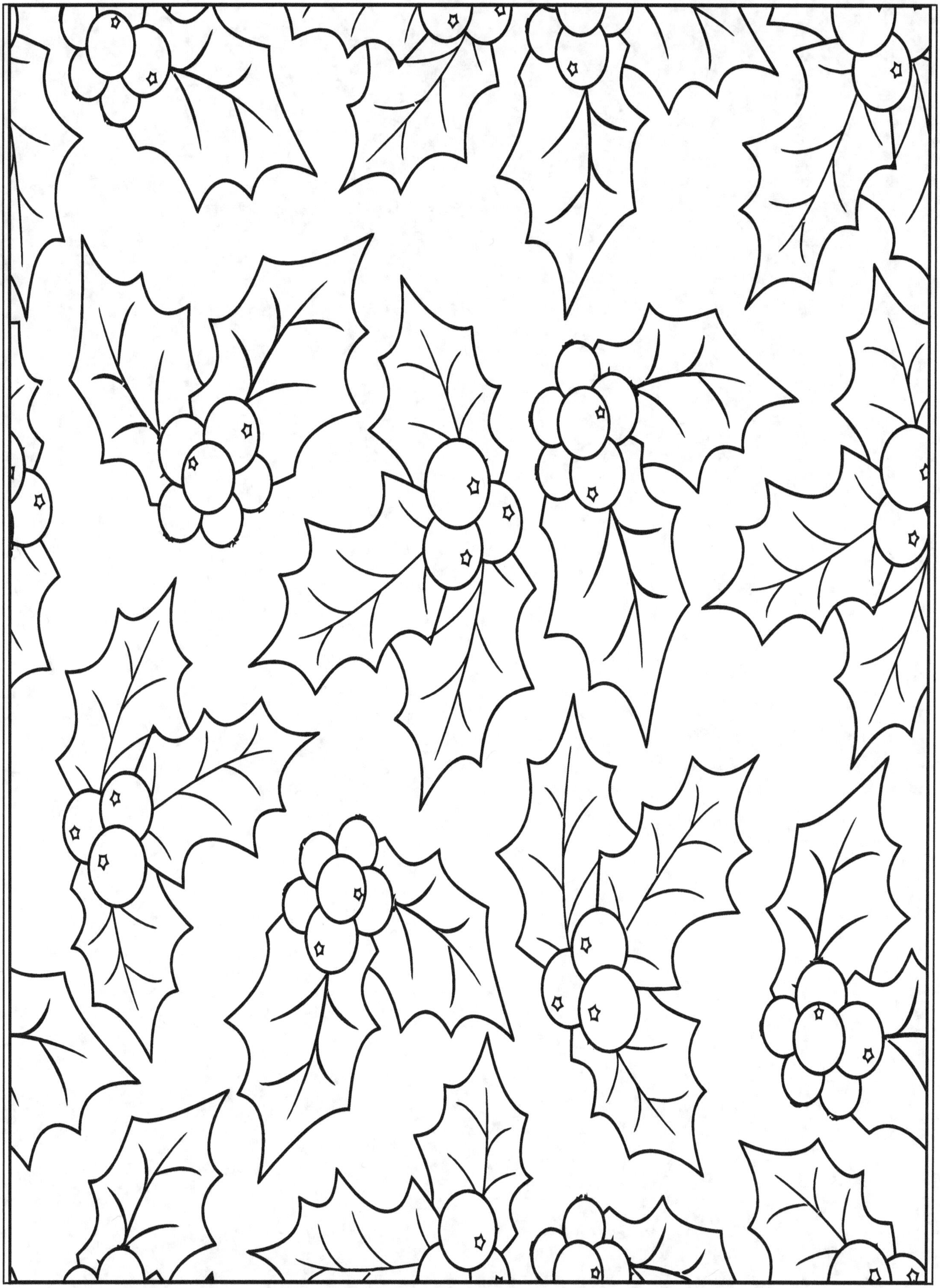

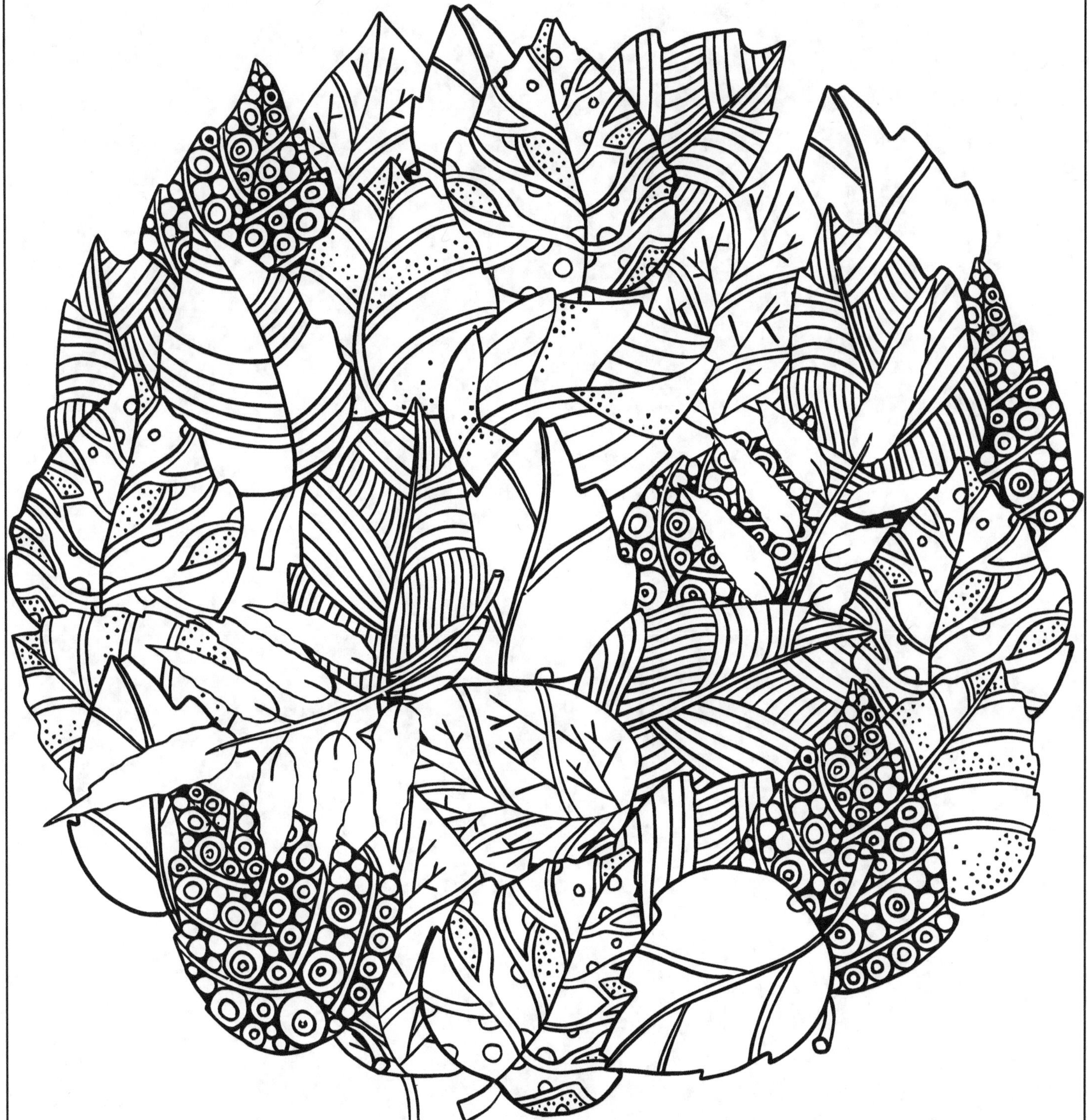

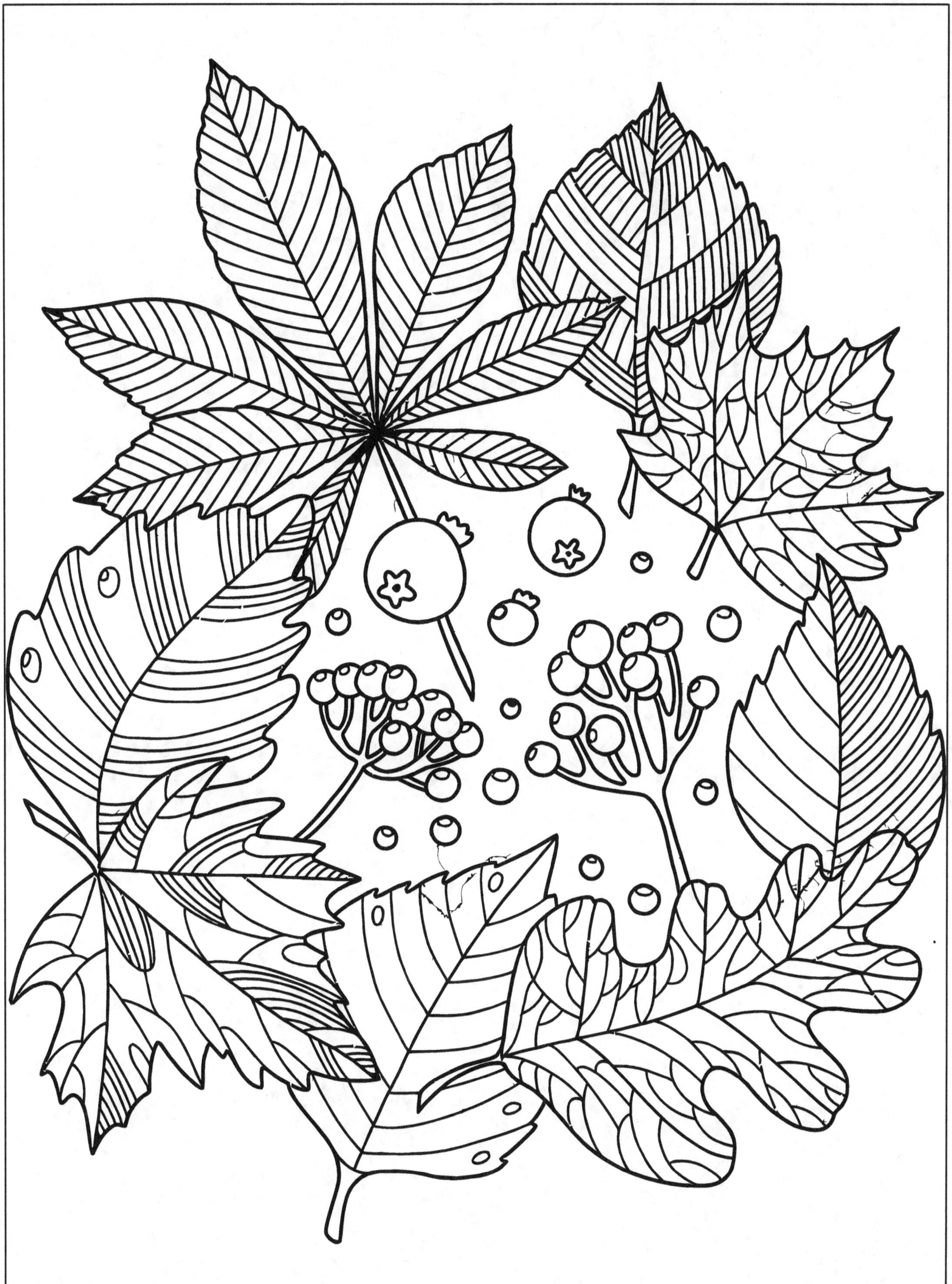

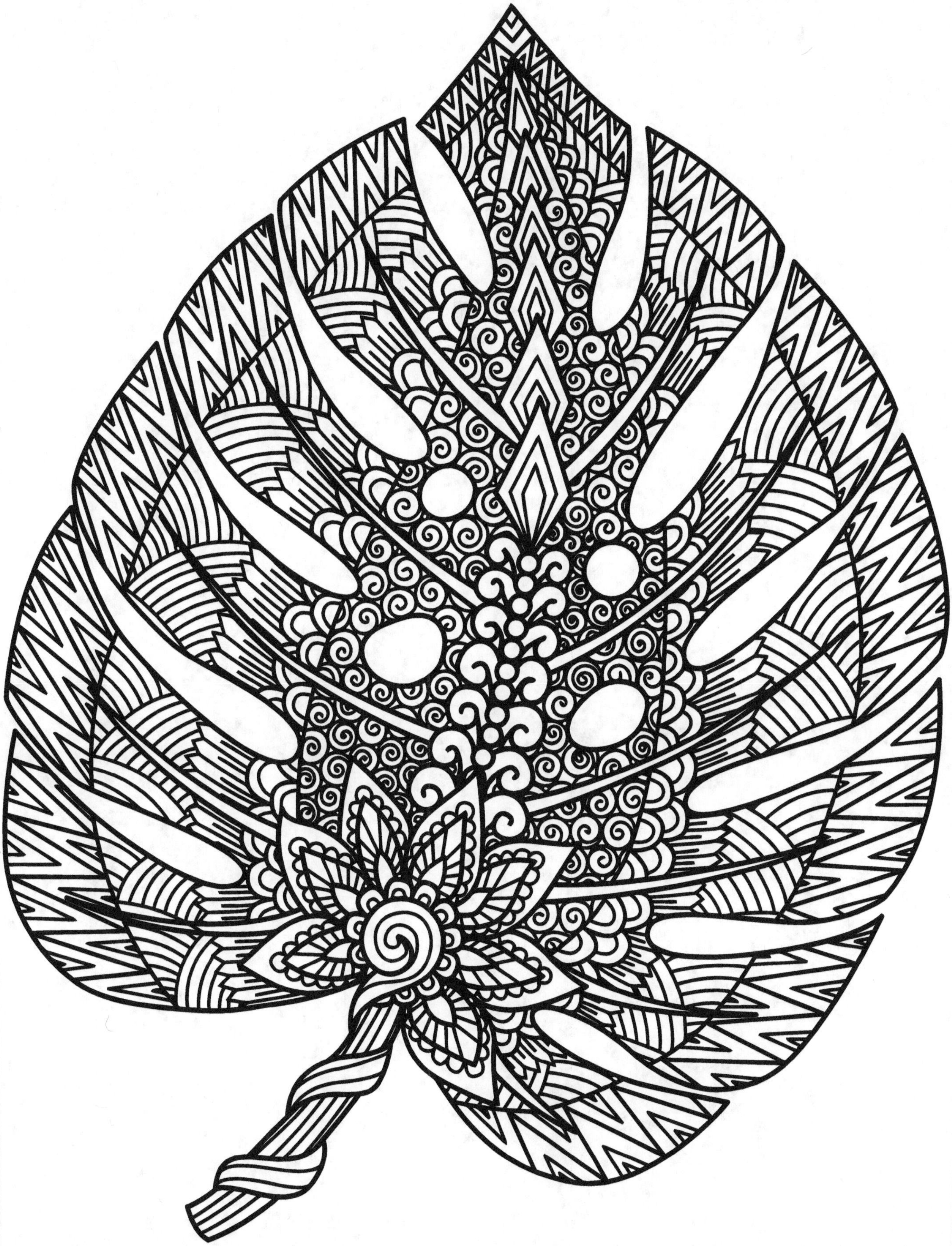

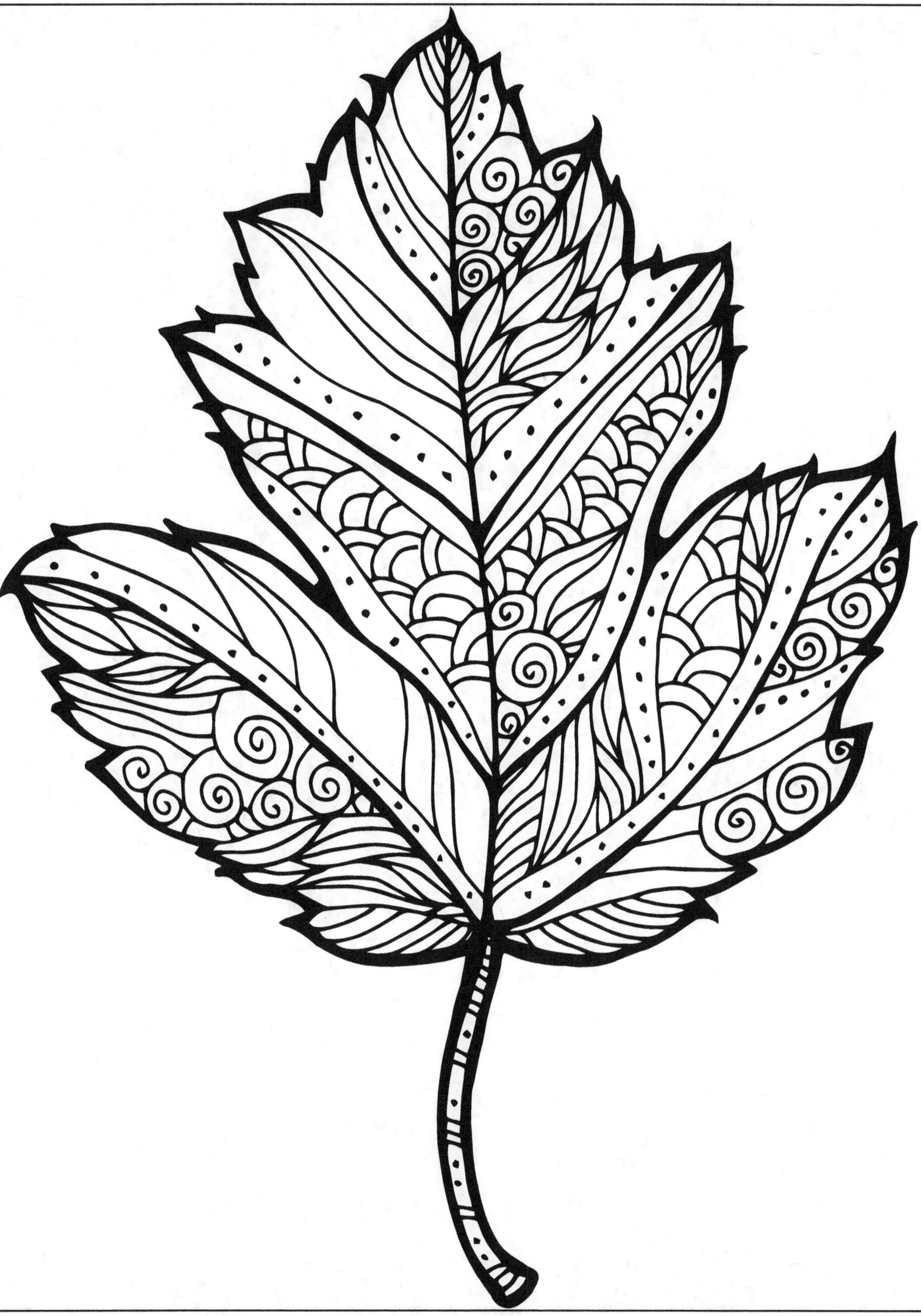

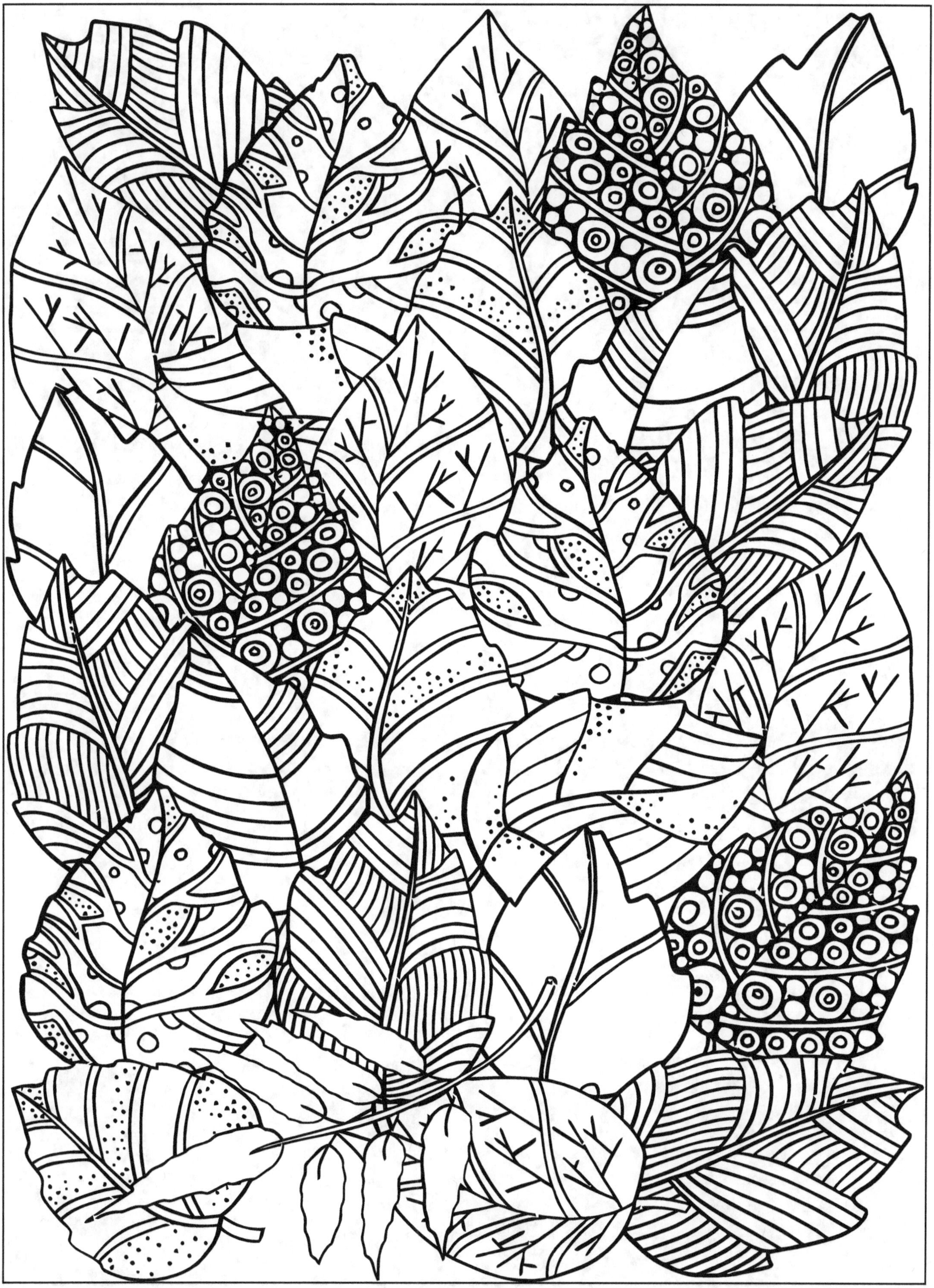

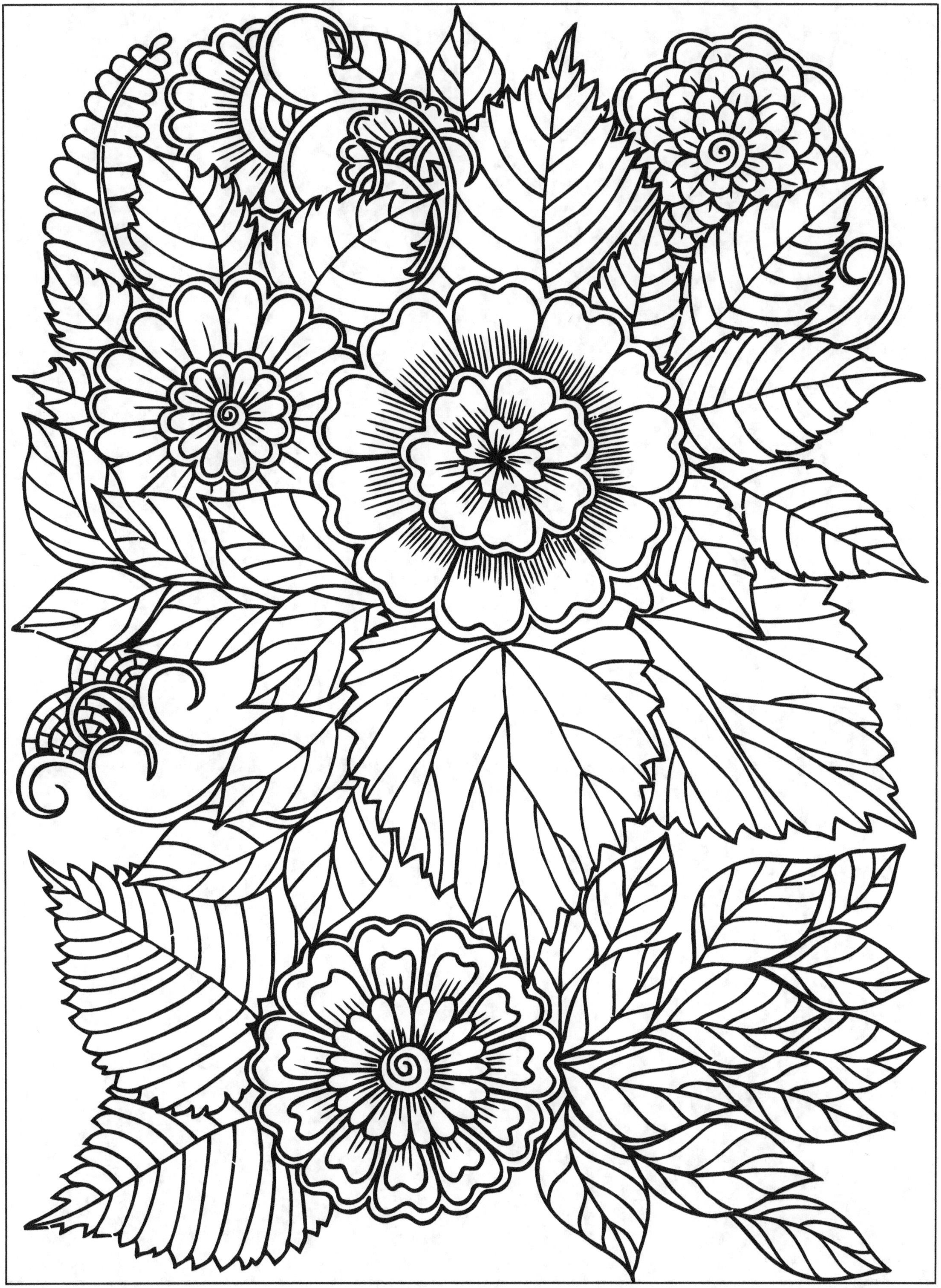

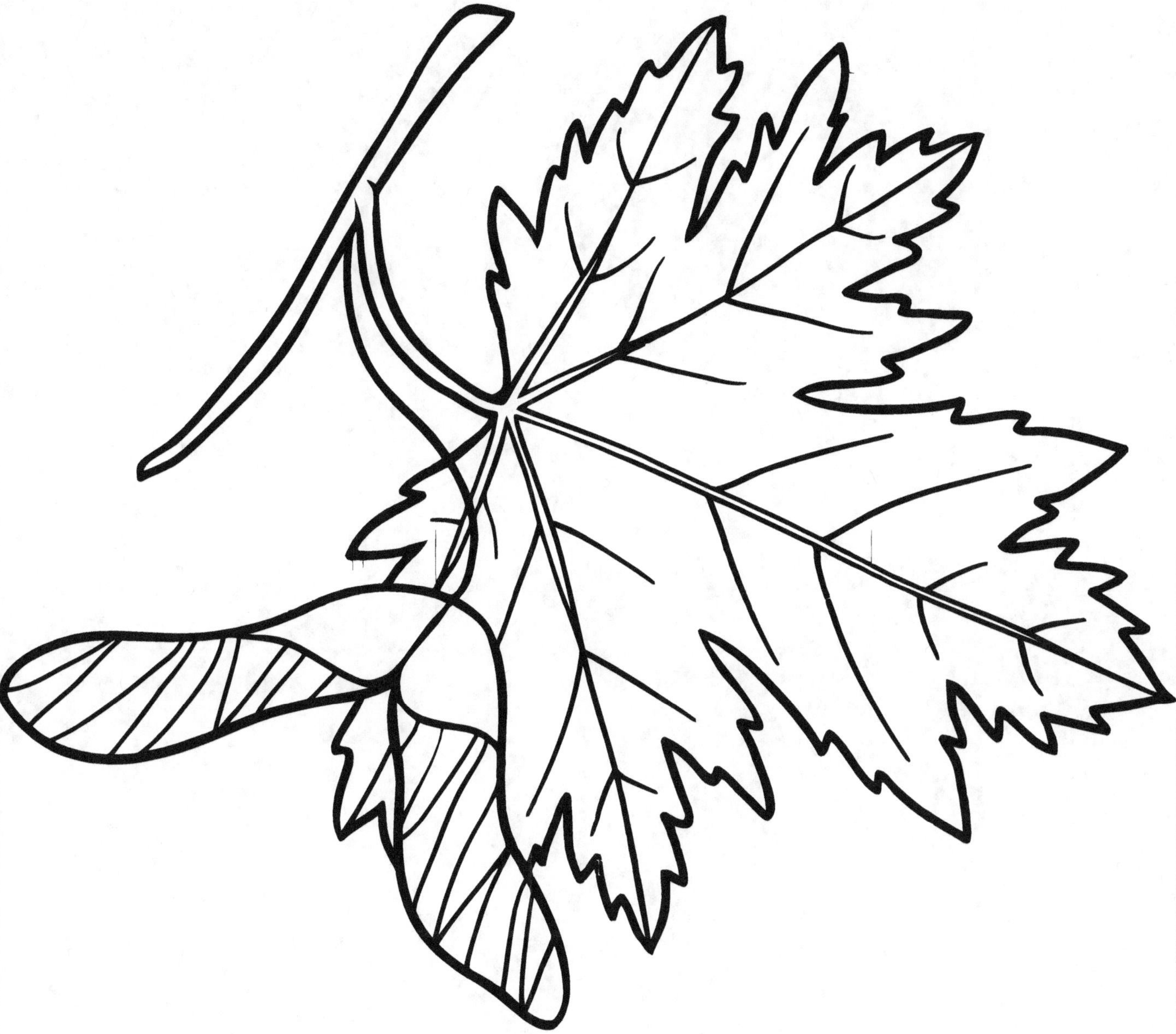

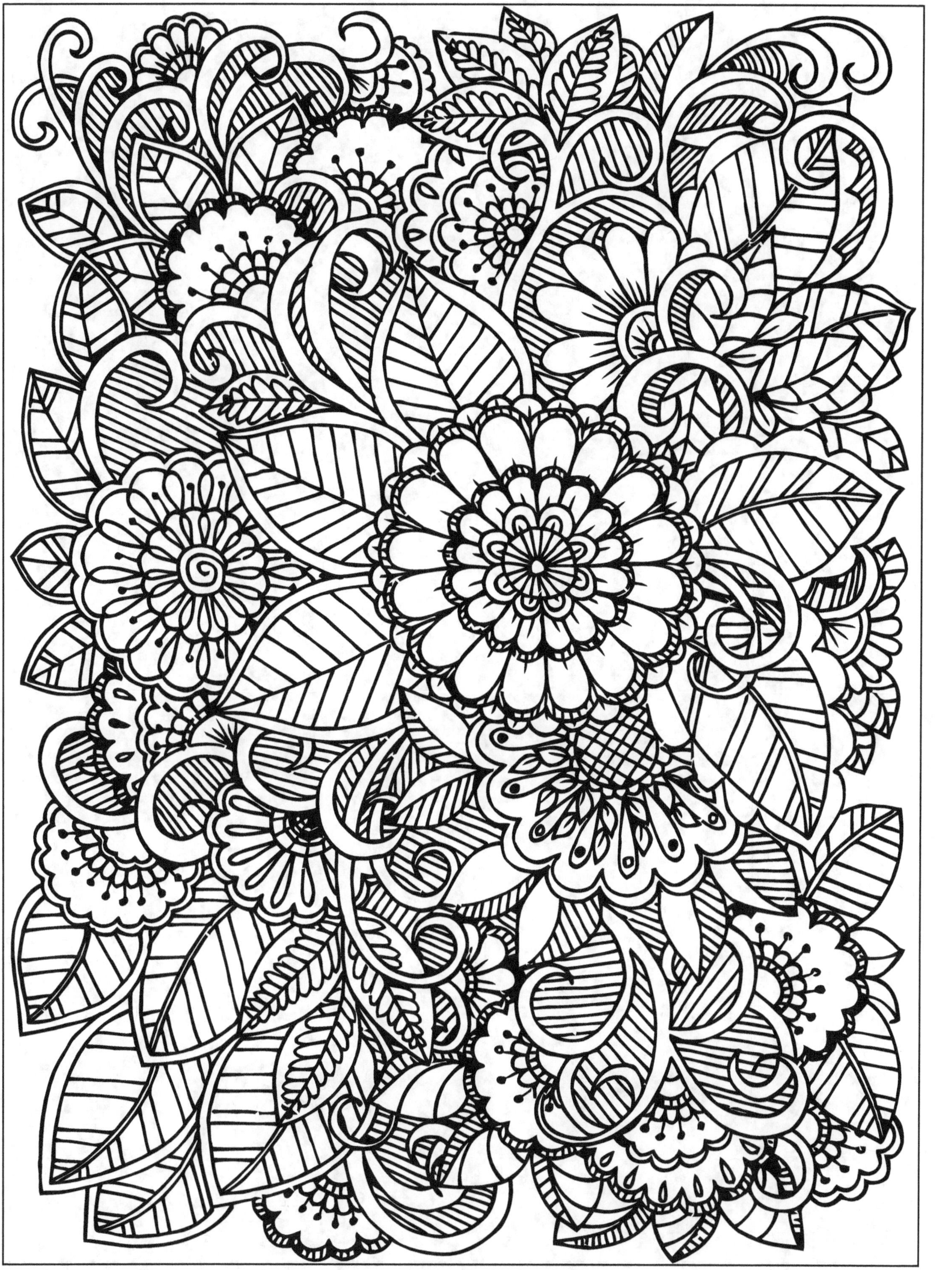

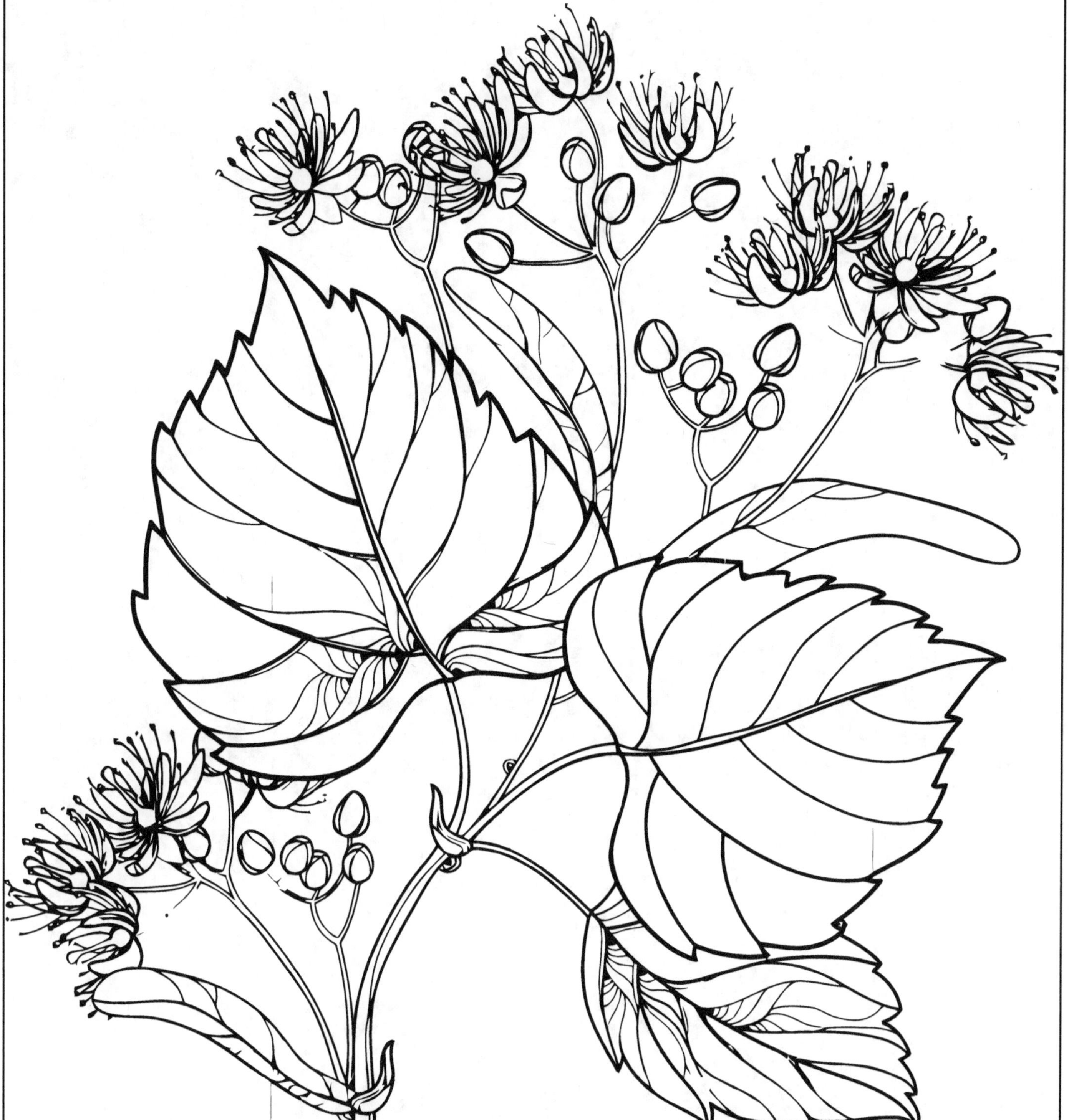

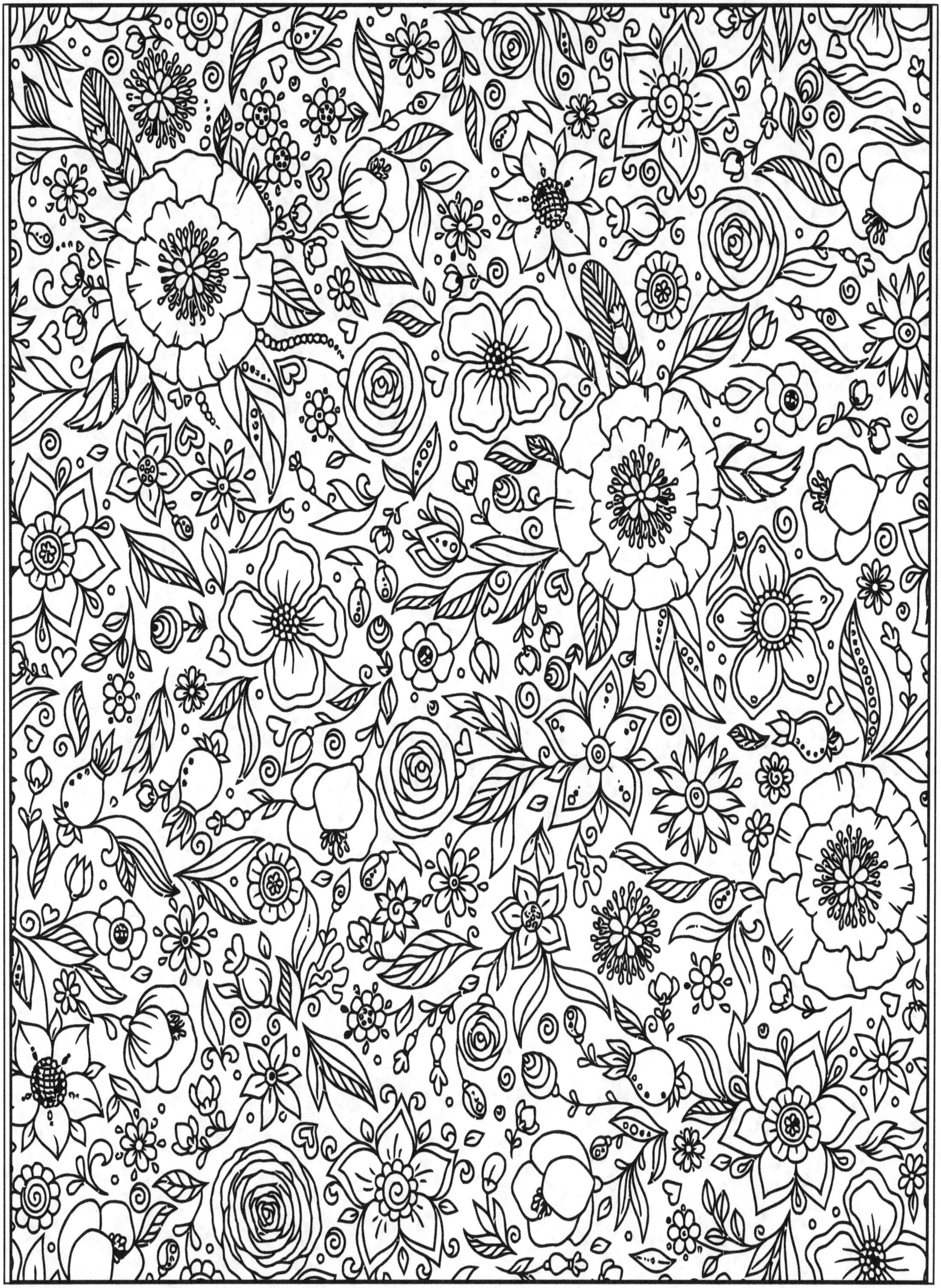

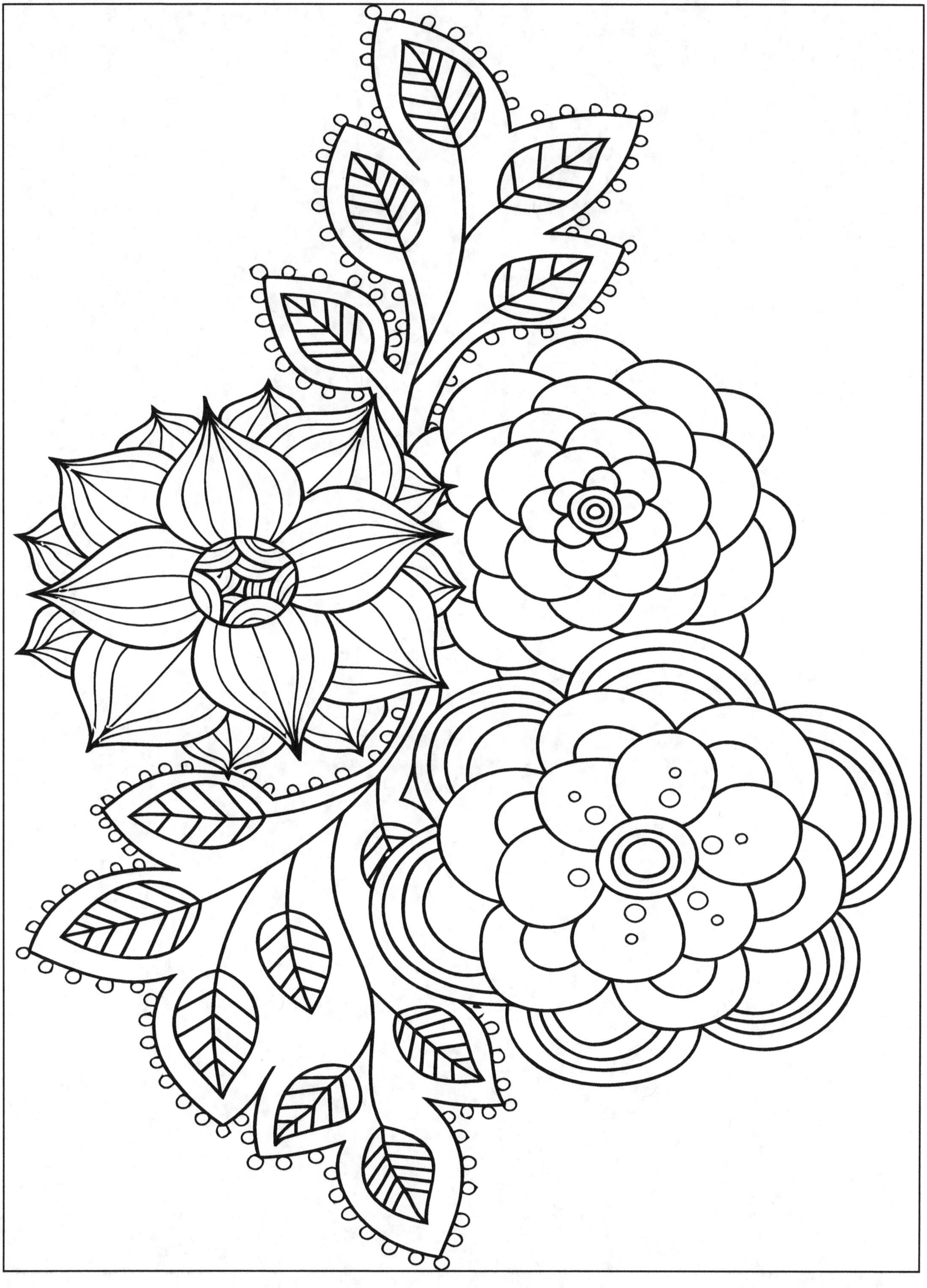

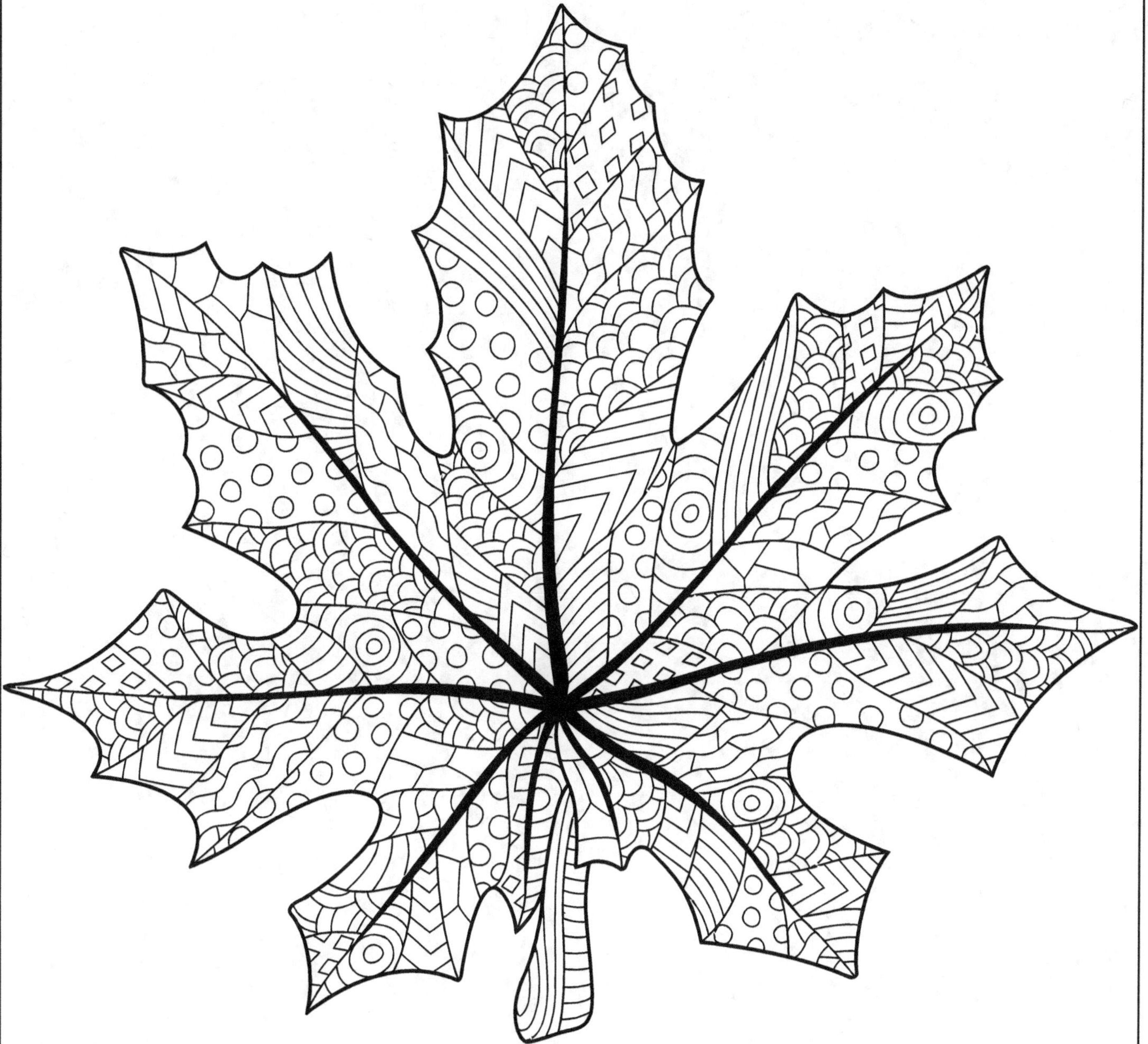

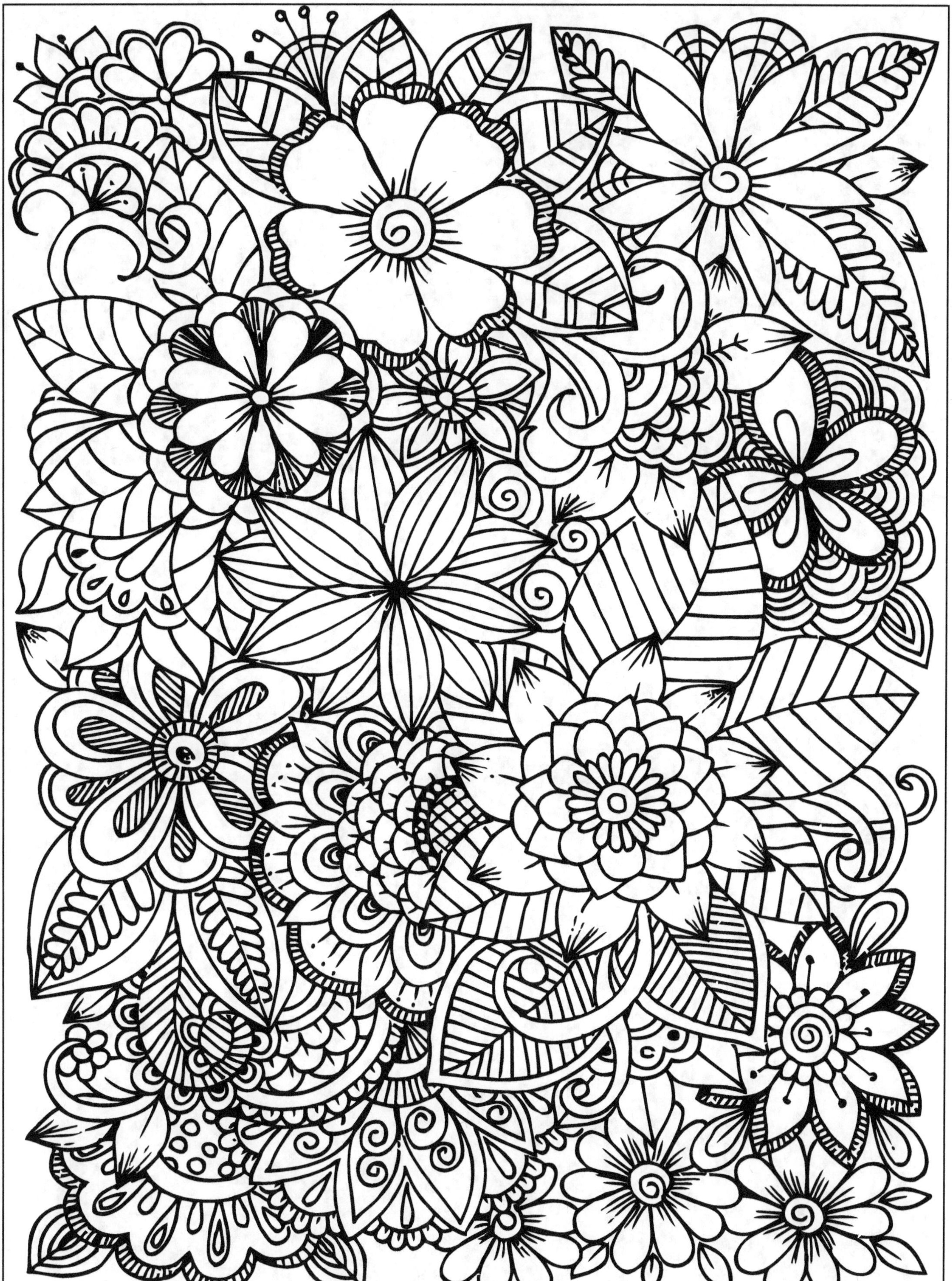

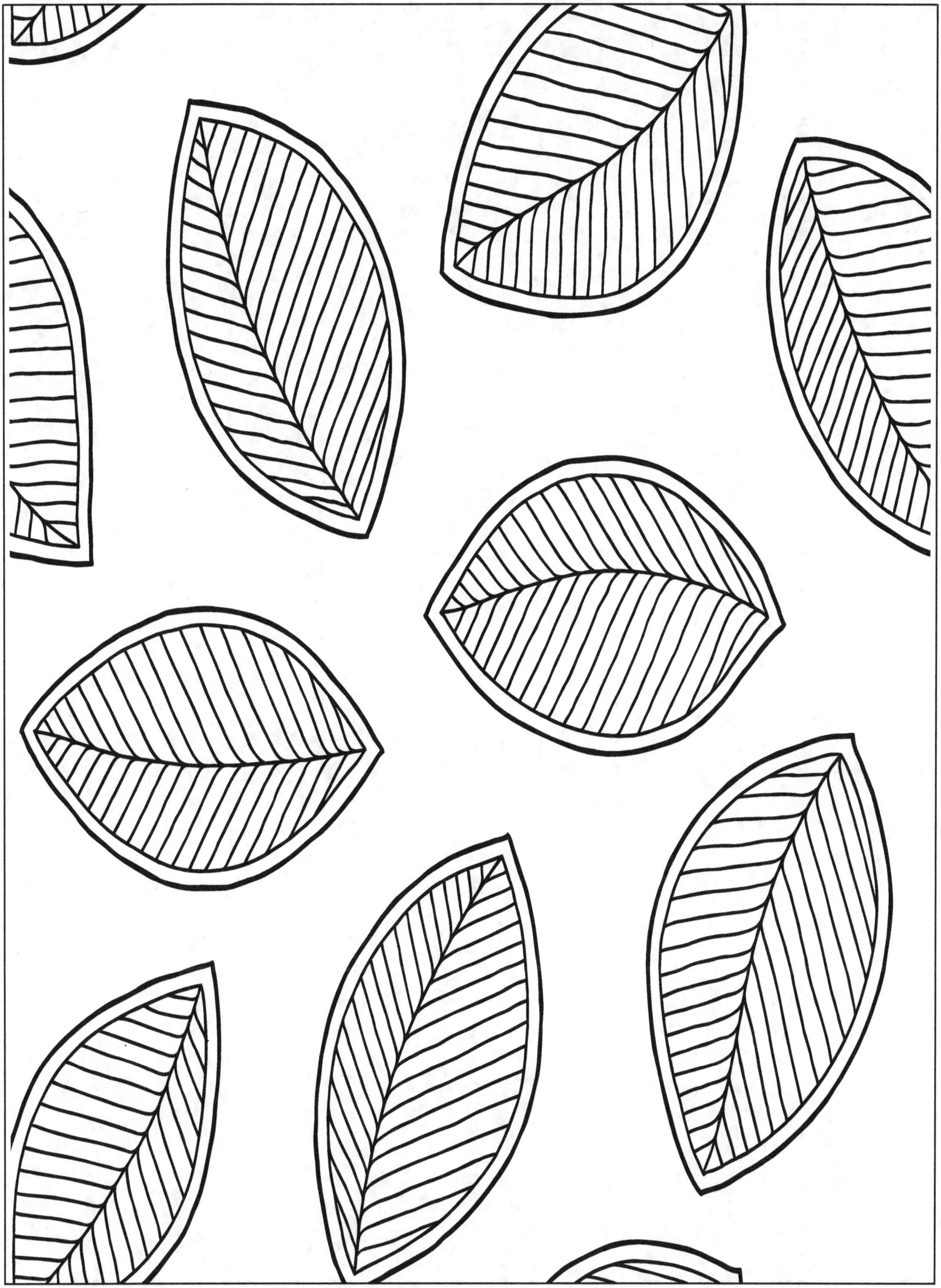

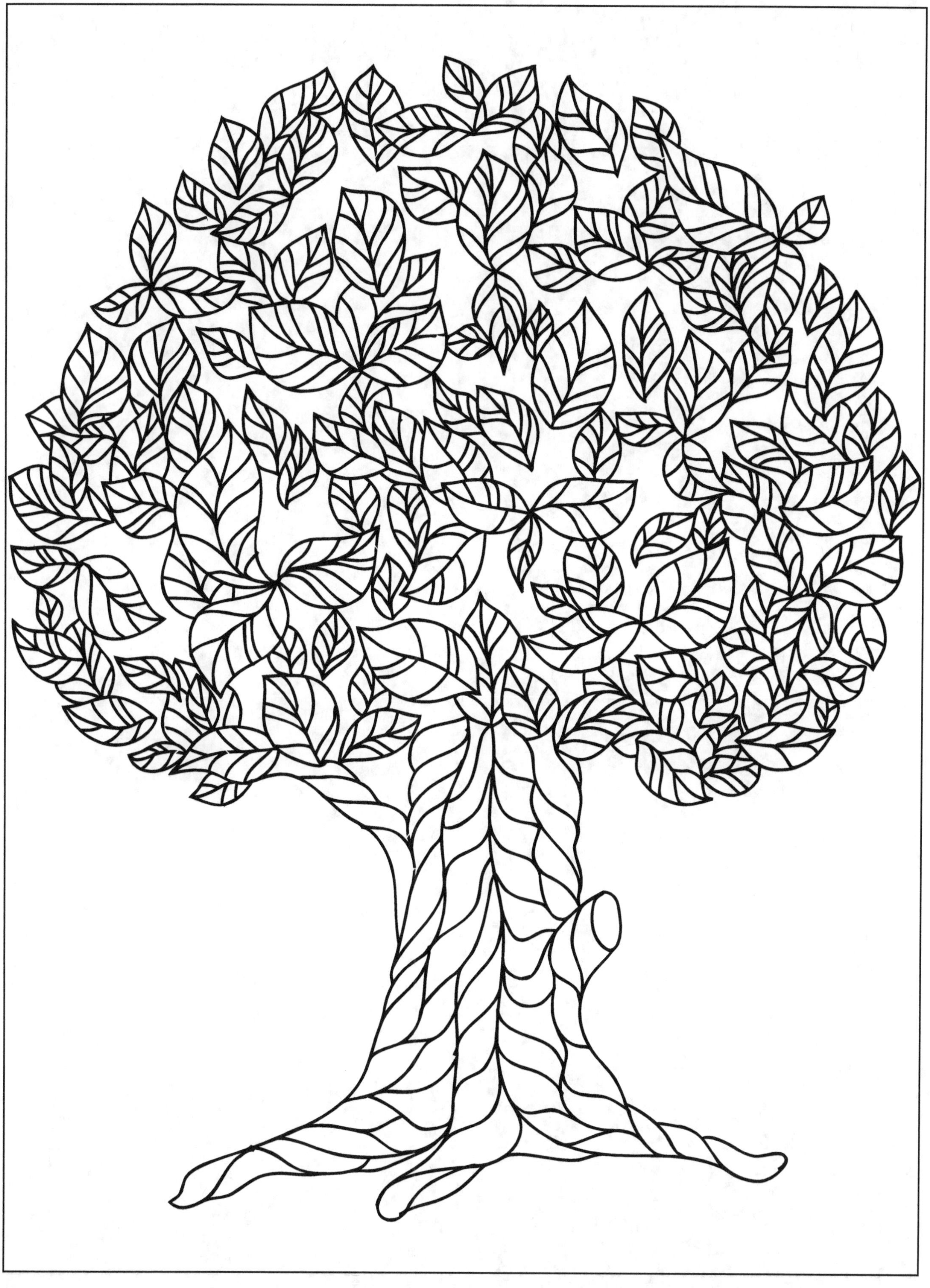

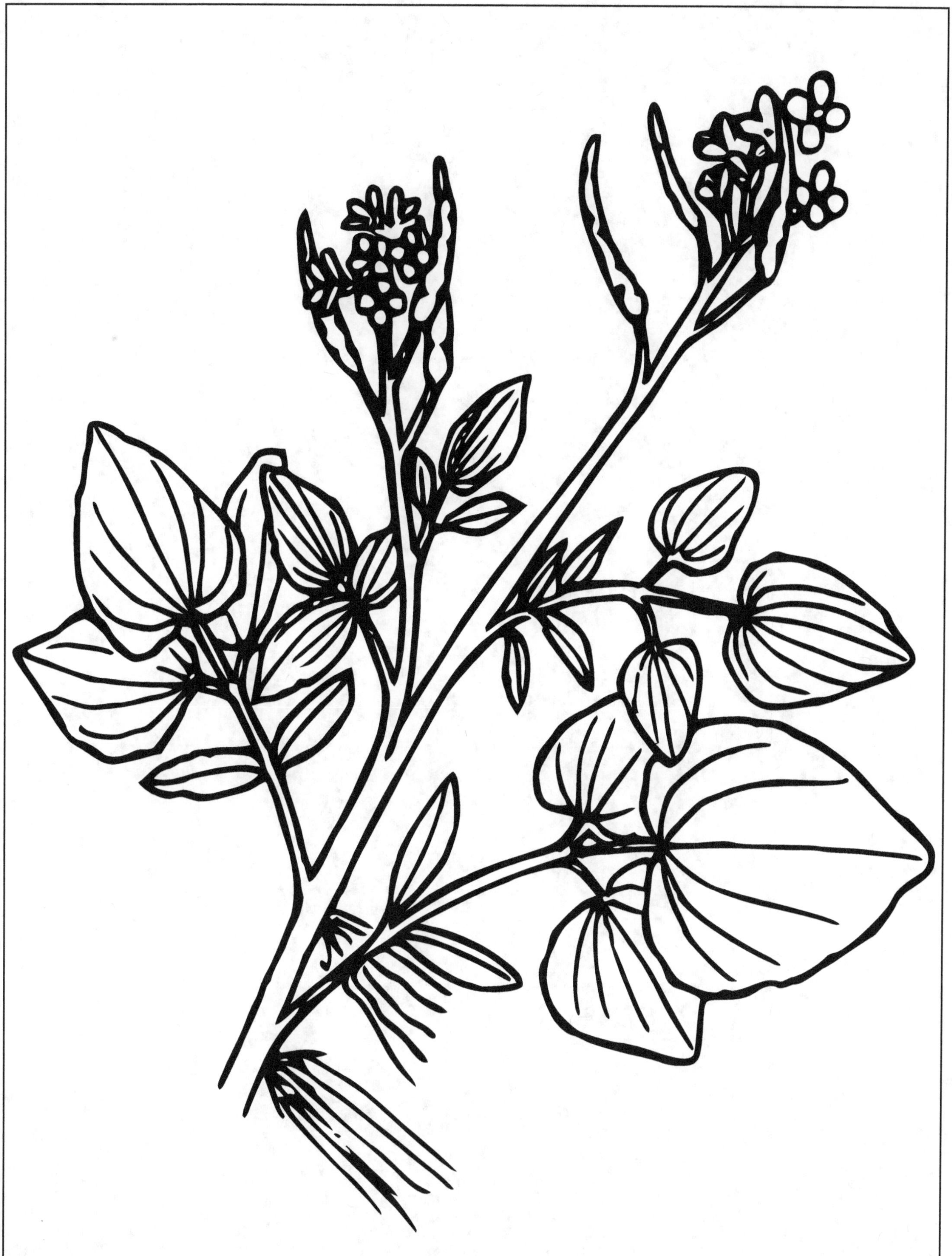

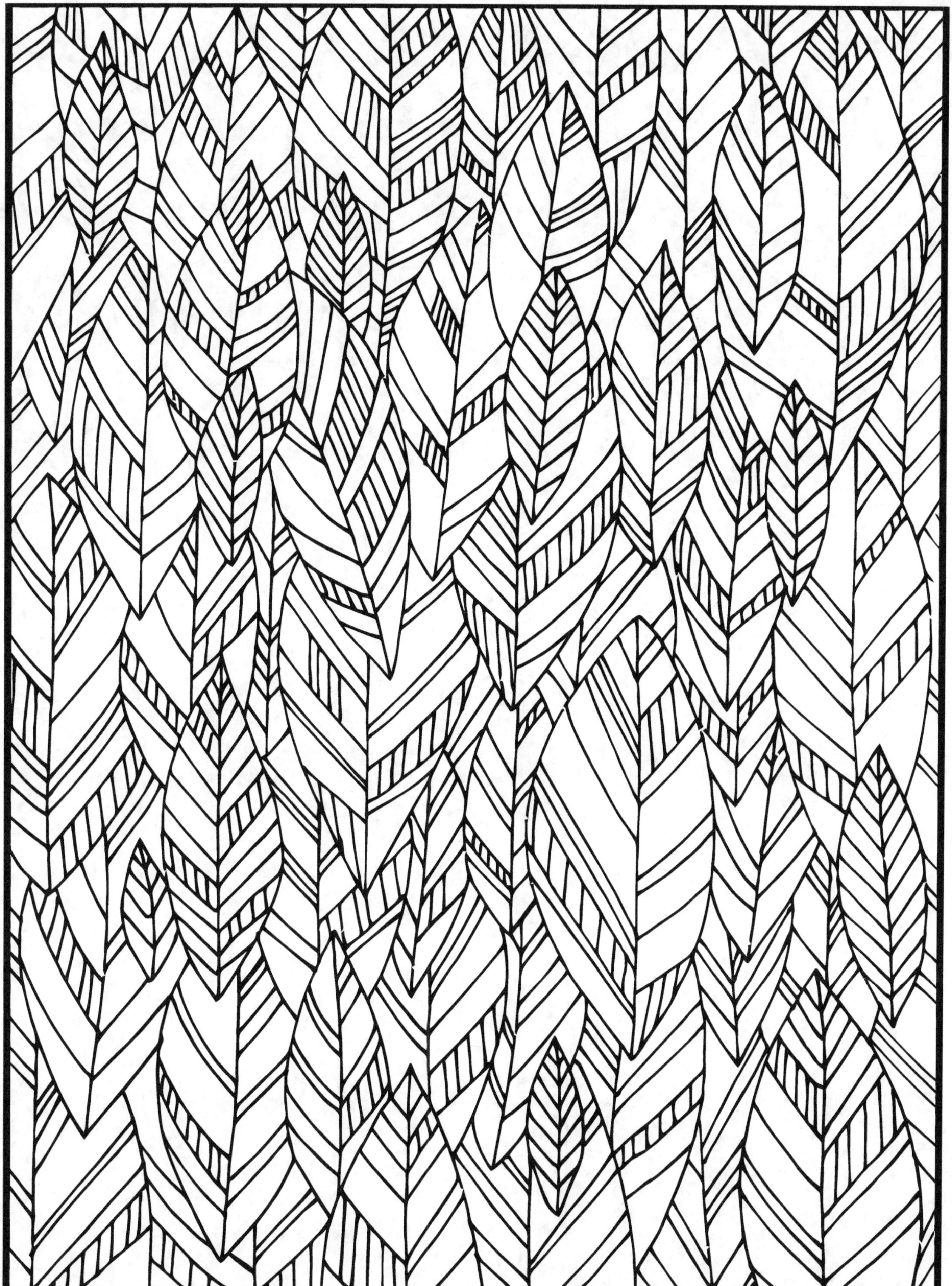

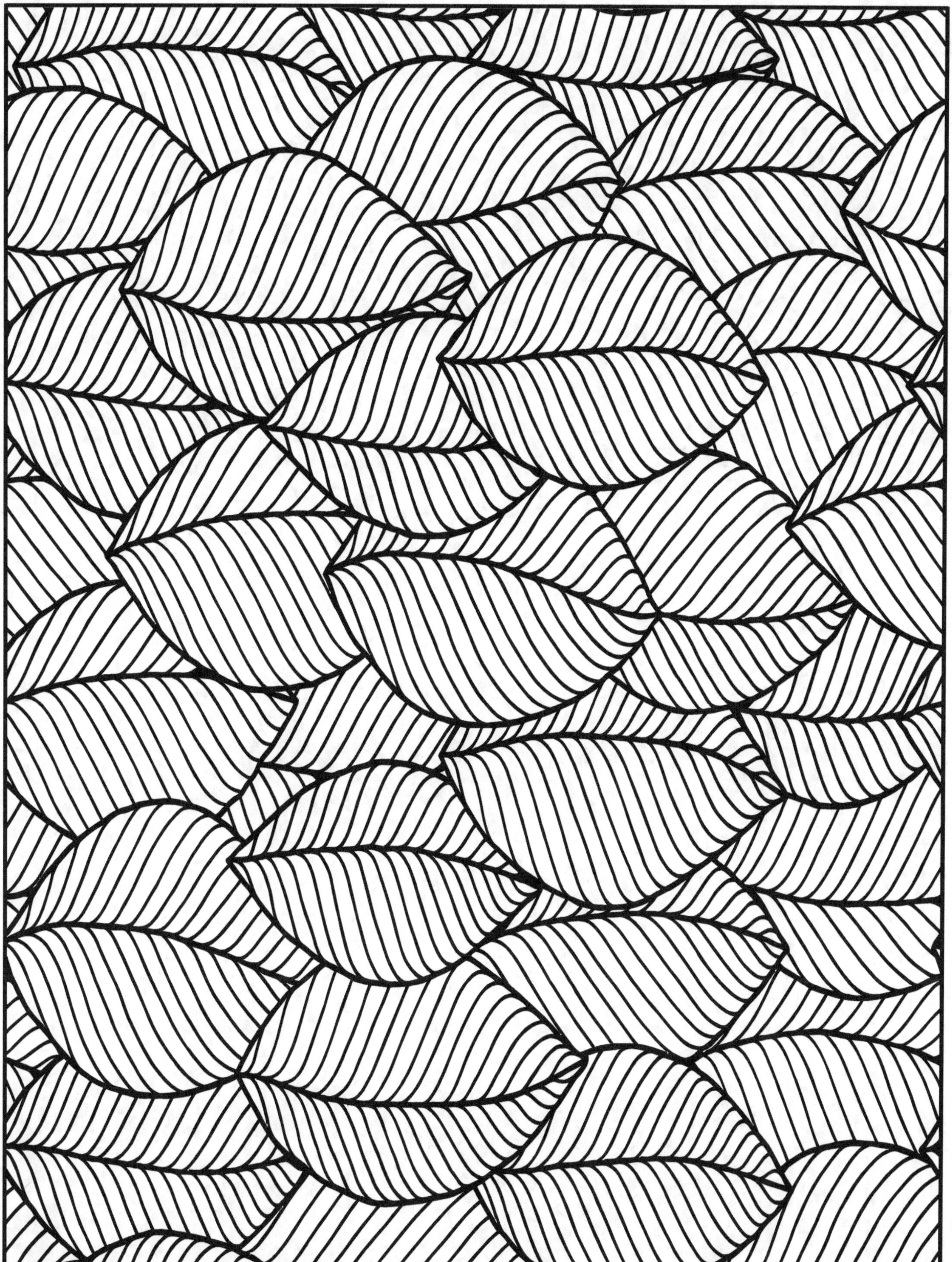

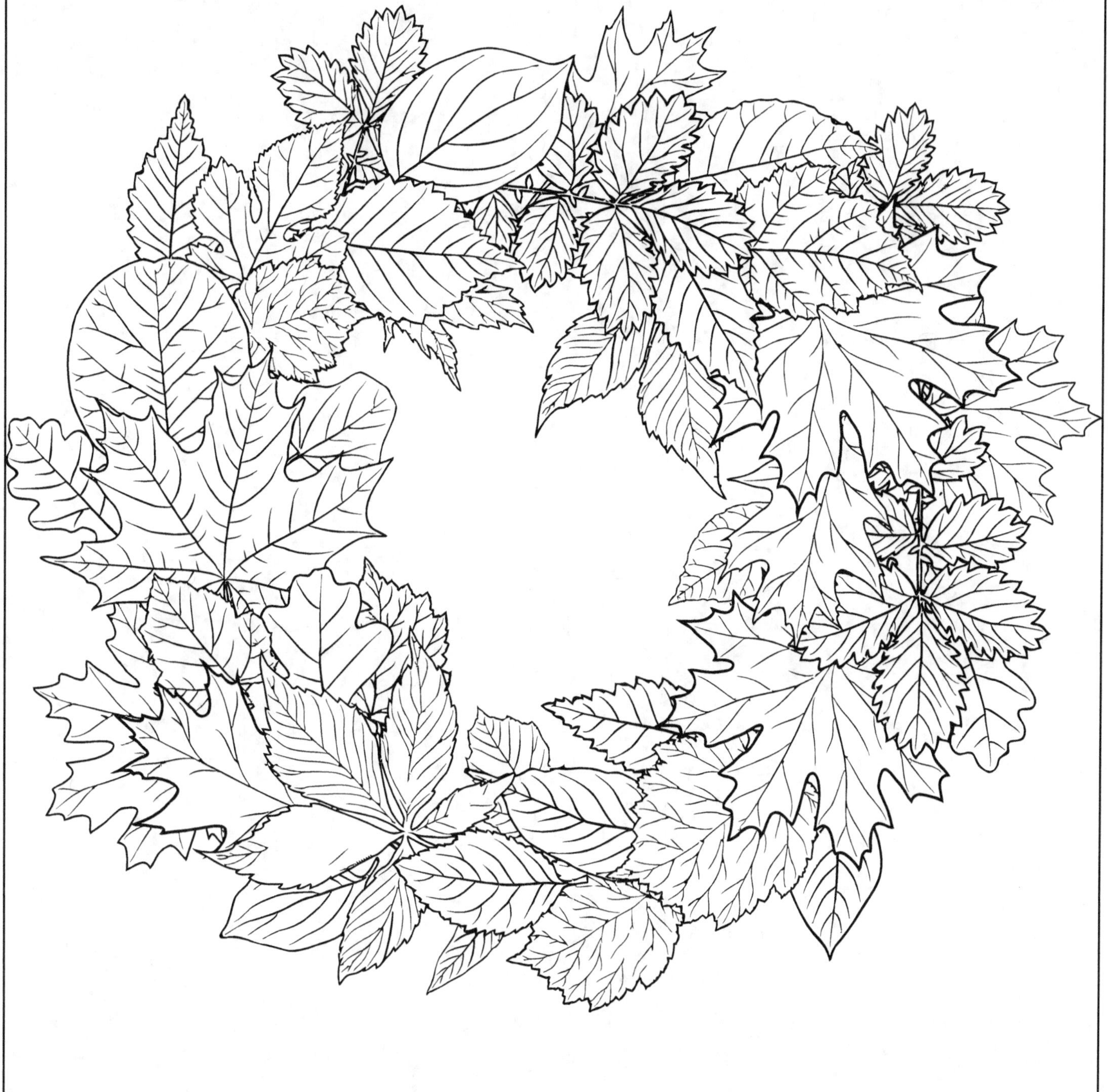

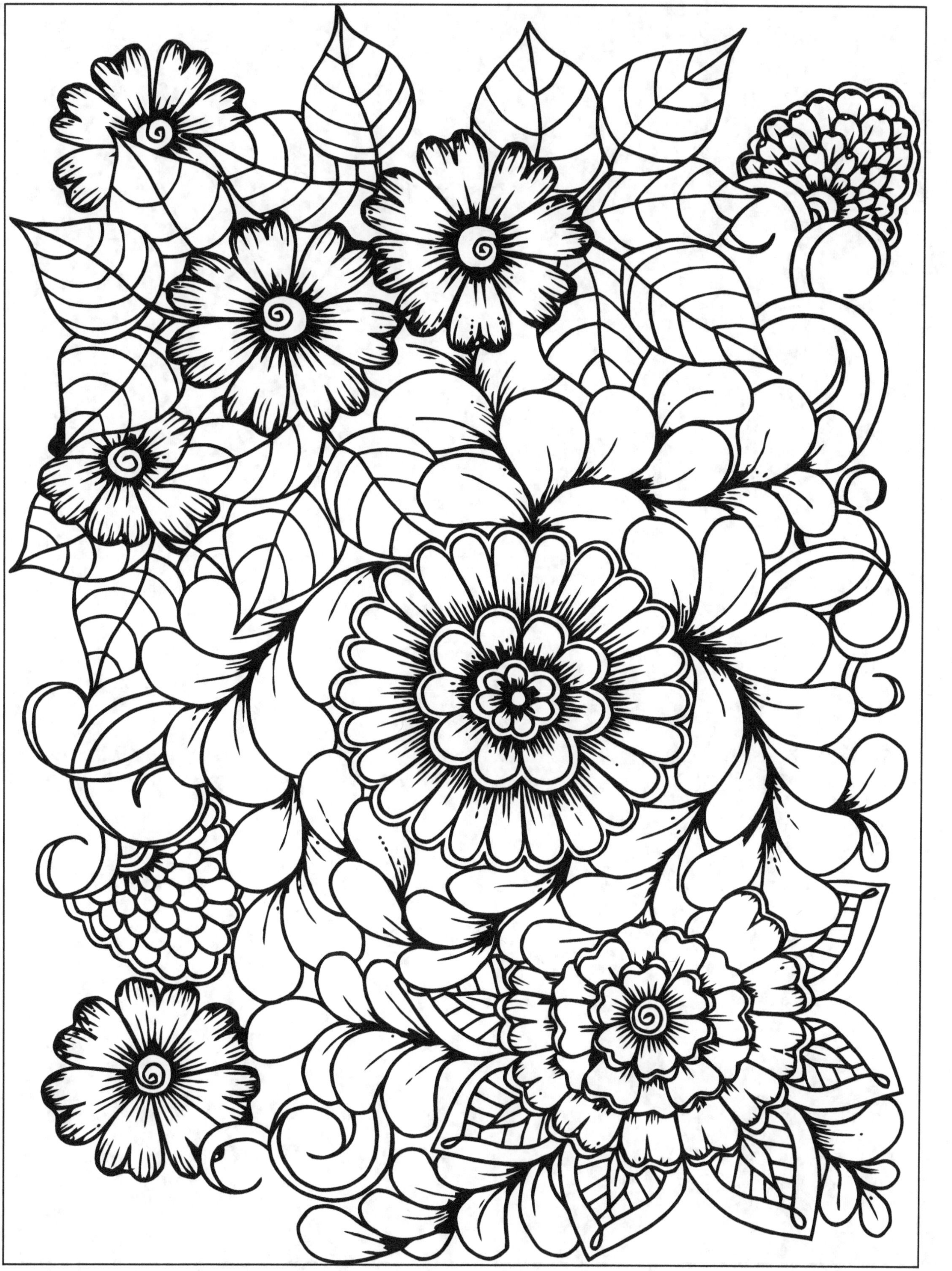

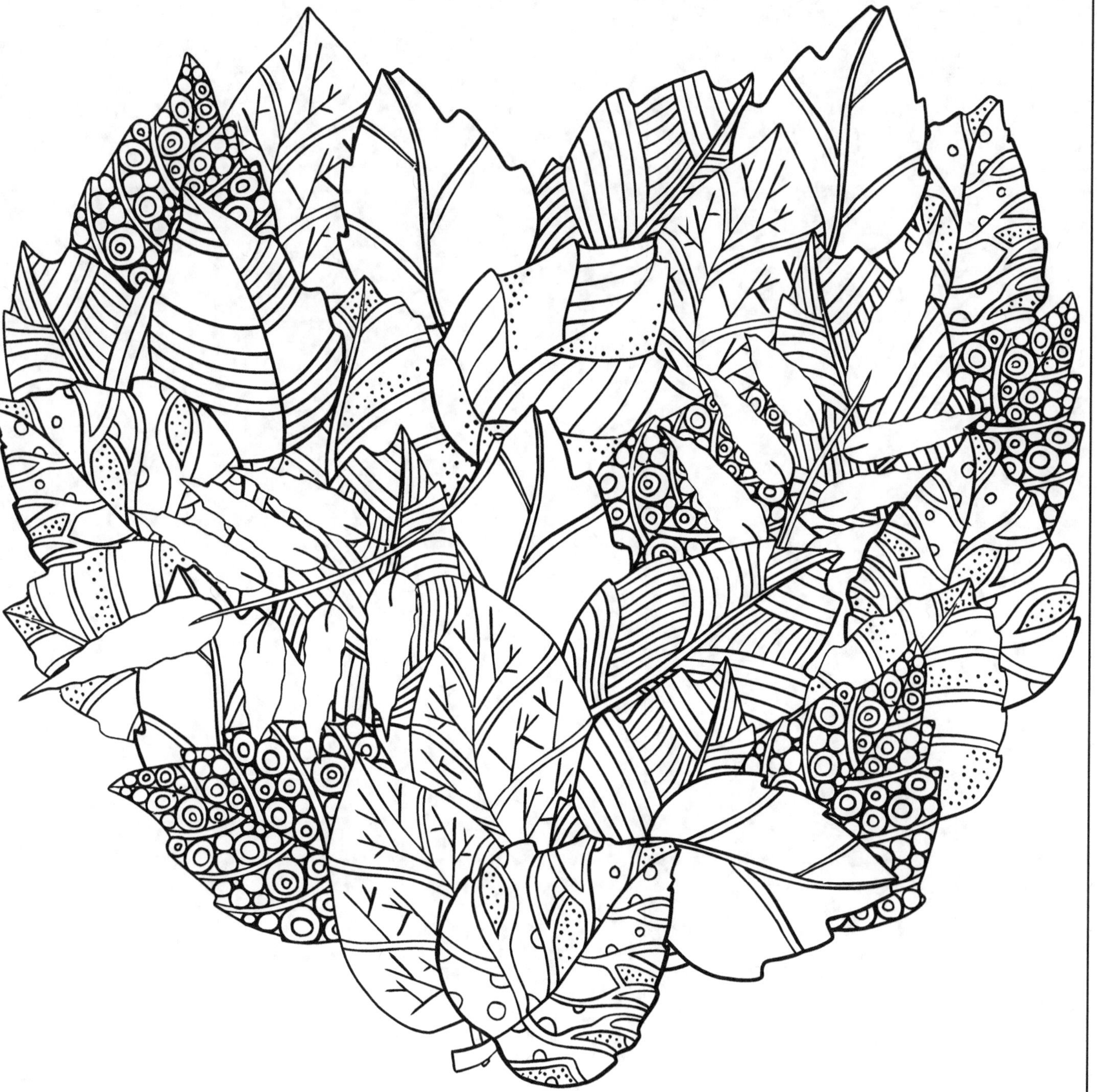

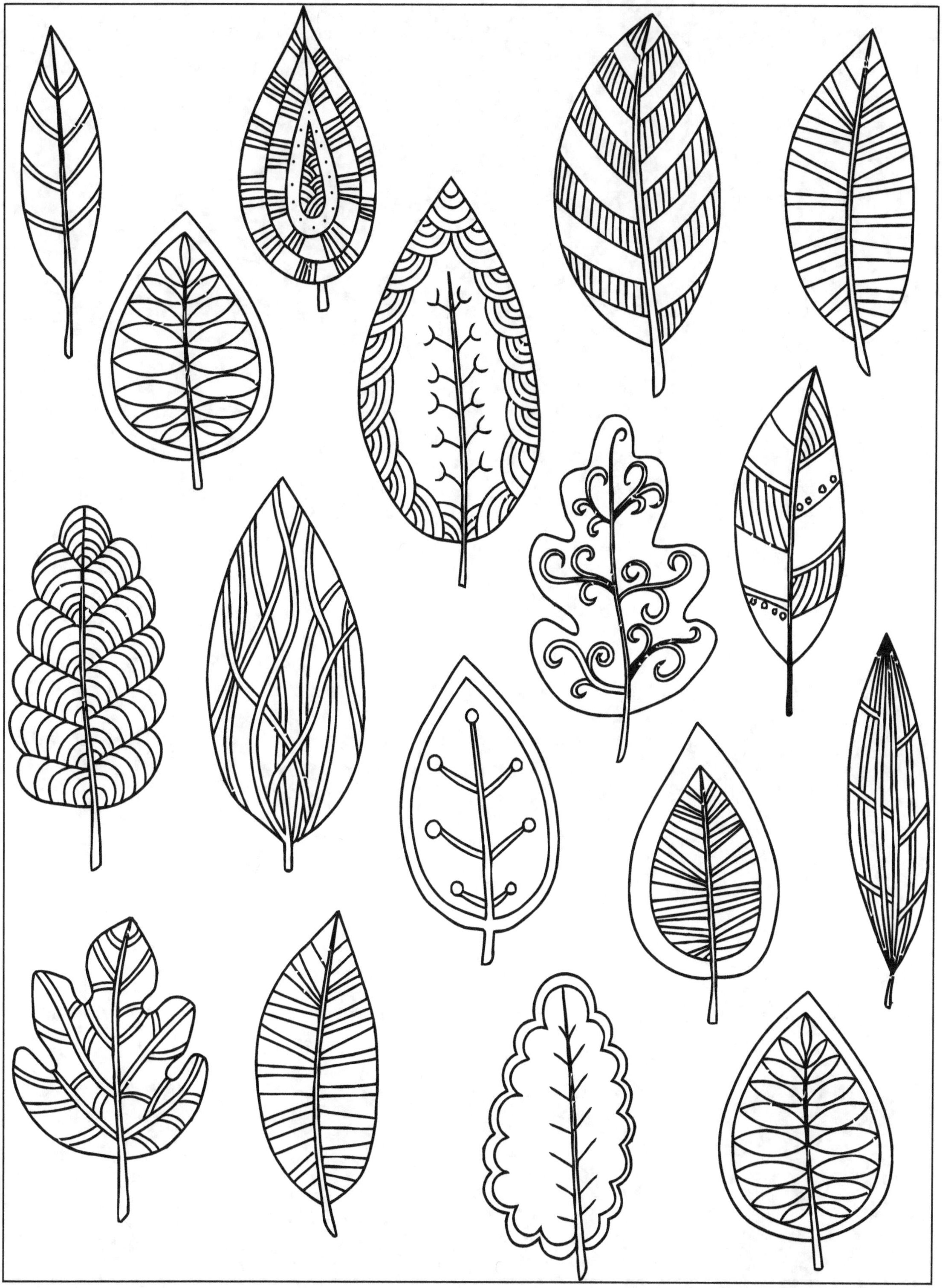

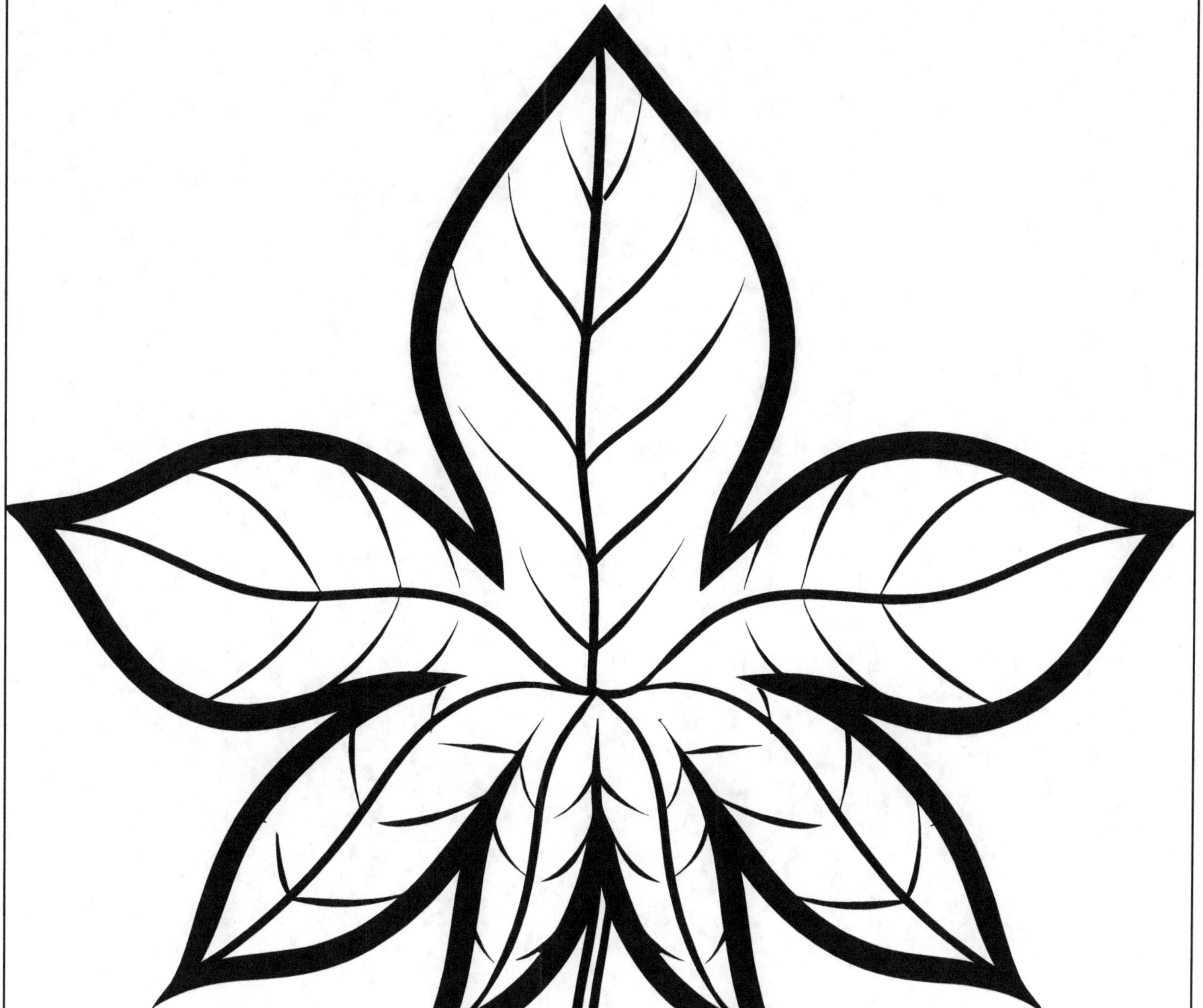

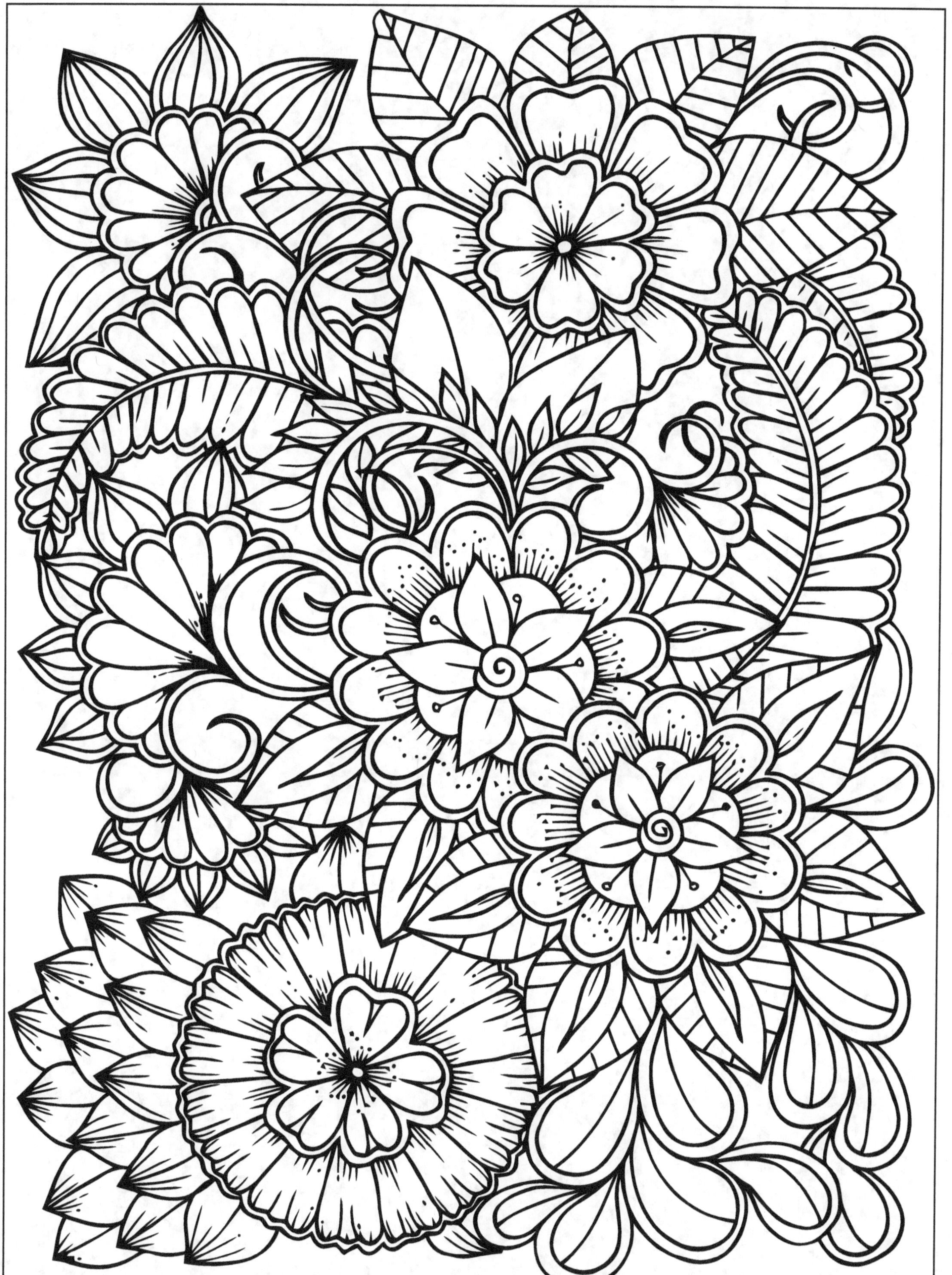

www.ingramcontent.com/pod-product-compliance
Lightning Source LLC
Chambersburg PA
CBHW082120220526
45472CB00009B/2247
* 9 7 9 8 4 1 9 5 9 4 6 3 0 *